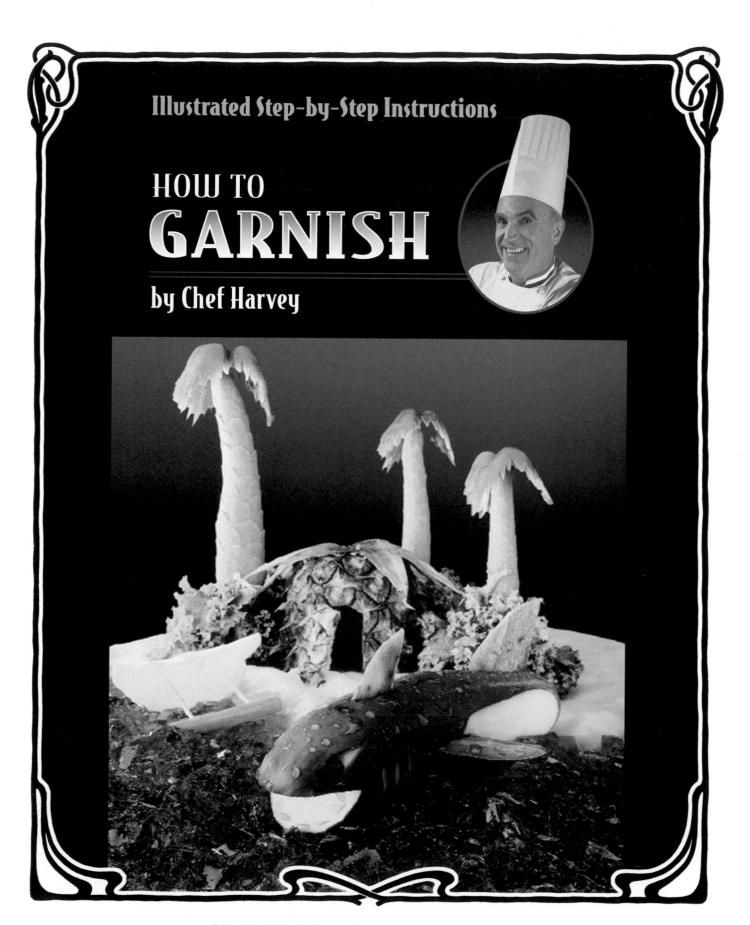

Illustrated Step-by-Step Instructions

HOW TO
GARNISH

by Chef Harvey

EDITED BY ROBERT J. ROSEN

Dedication

to the girls in my life...

Vicky • Rebecca Anne

Miranda Rose

Anne Aaron

Ann Melnick

Revised Edition

PUBLISHED BY:

INTERNATIONAL CULINARY

747 VASSAR AVENUE

LAKEWOOD, NEW JERSEY 08701 USA

CYBERSPACE ADDRESS:

E-MAIL: CHEFHARVEY@AOL.COM

WEBSITE: WWW.CHEFHARVEY.COM

International Culinary Consultants

Chef Harvey Rosen, G.M.

Chef Robert J. Rosen

Chef Jonathan S. Rosen

Chef Laurence M. Rosen

The International Culinary Consultants are known world-wide for their state-of-the-art publications and expertise in fine food presentation. They have appeared on local and national network television programs, are featured attractions at culinary expositions and tour extensively as promotional personalities.

Our staff is dedicated to the promotion of garde-manger through-out the world. If we can be of service to you please contact us.

Keffier V. Adkins
Art Director/Artist

Jeff Martin/*Photographic Assoc.*

COLOR PHOTOS

INDEX

Multiple Vegetable Garnishes

Dear Lover of Fine Food,

This book is an experience in garnishing. At your next party, you can impress your friends with your new discoveries. Your guests will not only enjoy your fine cooking but also will appreciate your garnishing artistry.

Encouraged by the overwhelming success of your fine cooking and garnishing ideas, you will continue to create sumptuous garnishes that inspire your guests to ask you to share your expertise with them.

Enjoy your newly discovered art form. When you combine the new garnishing skills this book will give you with the traditionally fine food you've always served, you'll have complete meals that *look* as good as they taste. And don't forget—what pleases the eye pleases the palate.

Harvey Rosen

Laurence Rosen

P.S.—A note to the beginner:

If this is your first exposure to *garde manger*, the term literally means "pantry" in French. This is the accepted culinary name for the art of food garnishing. There are a few things that should be kept in mind as you attempt your first few garnishes.

HAVE SOME PATIENCE.

Take your time. Work carefully, slowly and gently.

Follow the instructions closely and you too can duplicate my garnishes and centerpieces.

Although my book gives step-by-step instructions, you may alter the steps slightly.

The key is to be *creative!*

Be daring and experiment with your techniques—you may even develop your own unique garnish.

If you do create your own garnish and would like to share it with me and my readers, I invite you to contact me.

Garnishing Hints

While following the instructions for the garnishes, pay close attention to the hints that are included. The hints will in some cases make the difference between a successful, attractive garnish and an unsuccessful one.

Following is a collection of garnishing hints that are quite helpful in *garde manger* work.

- Many of the garnishes require soaking in ice water.
  The ice water makes the vegetables rigid and allows sliced sections to separate and curl.
  Ice water is also an excellent medium for preserving garnishes for a few days.

- **Certain garnishes require a pliable vegetable slice that can be bent or curled without breaking.**
  This can be accomplished by soaking the slices in a saltwater solution (2 tbs. salt in 1 pt. water) until the desired flexibility is achieved.

- **Coat fruits and vegetables with clear gelatin to preserve them and to give them an attractive shine.**

- **Lemon juice has a variety of uses.**
  It can be used to prevent an apple slice from darkening and to remove the onion odor from hands.
  Lemon juice acts as a preservative when used to coat fruits and vegetables.
  If lemon juice is not available, crush two vitamin C tablets in a small bowl of water and coat your garnishes with this solution.

- **To preserve garnishes for a longer period of time, submerge them in water and store them in the freezer.**
  The garnishes stored in ice will stay fresh for 8 to 10 months. This is a convenient way to have a fresh garnish at your disposal whenever you need it.

- Most garnishes can be made in advance.
  This comes in handy, since your time will be limited on the day of your party and you will not have the extra time to go slowly and carefully enough to ensure perfectly formed garnishes.
  Store beet, carrot, turnip, radish, onion, pepper, and celery garnishes in ice water.

Simply refrigerate garnishes made from cucumbers, eggplants, tomatoes, citrus fruits, melons, and apples. (Apples should also be coated with lemon juice.)

When making watermelon sculptures, store the fruit salad made from the melon and other fruits in a sealed container. The watermelon shell can be preserved by placing some ice inside and replacing the rind to seal the shell. (Set this in a cool place.) If the rind can not be replaced, simply wrap the watermelon in a good plastic food wrap and refrigerate.

- **Proper equipment should be used at all times for each operation!**
  Be sure that all knives are sharp and free from rust. To ensure safe handling, store all sharp knives in a cardboard sheath.

- **Soaking an onion or scallion in hot water with lemon for approximately 5 minutes can remove the odor. Then soak in ice water.**

- **Toothpicks and wooden skewers are essential elements in *garde-manger* work.**
  They are used extensively to attach food sections to one another.

- **Floral tape may be used to secure and support vegetables.**

- **When presenting certain garnishes, a slice of raw potato can be used as a base for support.**
  Cover the potato with greens (or red cabbage) and attach the garnish with toothpicks.

- **To give garnishes an artistic flair, craft supplies (plastic eyes, pussy willows, baby's breath, colored leaves, etc.) may be added.**
  Do *not* rely on the artificial addition to carry the garnish; use it only to enhance the garnish, not to overpower it.

- **Use food coloring to give garnishes a variety of colors.**
  It is best to mix the dye with water in a small glass and dip the garnish into the solution to color it. Always remove the excess dye by shaking or spinning it. For more brilliant colors, allow the garnish to soak in the solution for a longer period of time.

- **Arrange vegetable platters, cheese trays, and centerpieces on a bed of greens, chicory, escarole, Romaine lettuce, or curly endive.**
  When placing the garnishes on the tray, symmetry is the key. Place one large garnish in the center with vegetables or other food around it or place a few garnishes in a symmetrical pattern.
  Do not clutter the tray with food. Instead, make two or three platters with food spread out nicely.

- **Determine the ripeness of a watermelon by its color.**
  A yellowish underside, regardless of the rich green color of the rest of the melon, is a good sign of ripeness. "Thumping" a melon for ripeness is often misleading.

- **Carrots, beets, and turnips are popular vegetables for garnishes, but special care must be taken with them.**
  Select thick large vegetables and work with them at room temperature.
  Cold vegetables, especially carrots, are brittle and have a tendency to split.

- **Select fruits and vegetables that will best suit the garnish to be made.**
  Tall, thin onions produce better onion mums than short, squat ones; larger scallions are best for flowers; thicker carrots are easier to work with.
  In general, fruits and vegetables should be of uniform shape, and without blemishes or bruises.
  Choose fresh ripe fruits and vegetables that are crisp and have bright color.
  All vegetables should be washed and dried before carving. They should never be frozen before working with them.

HOW TO GARNISH

Culinary Tools

The following equipment will aid you in creating the garnishes described in this book. Some are elaborate, while others are very basic. They are all designed to save you time and energy in your work as a *garde-manger* chef.

If you can not locate this equipment in a store near you, you may contact the publisher of this book for purchasing information.

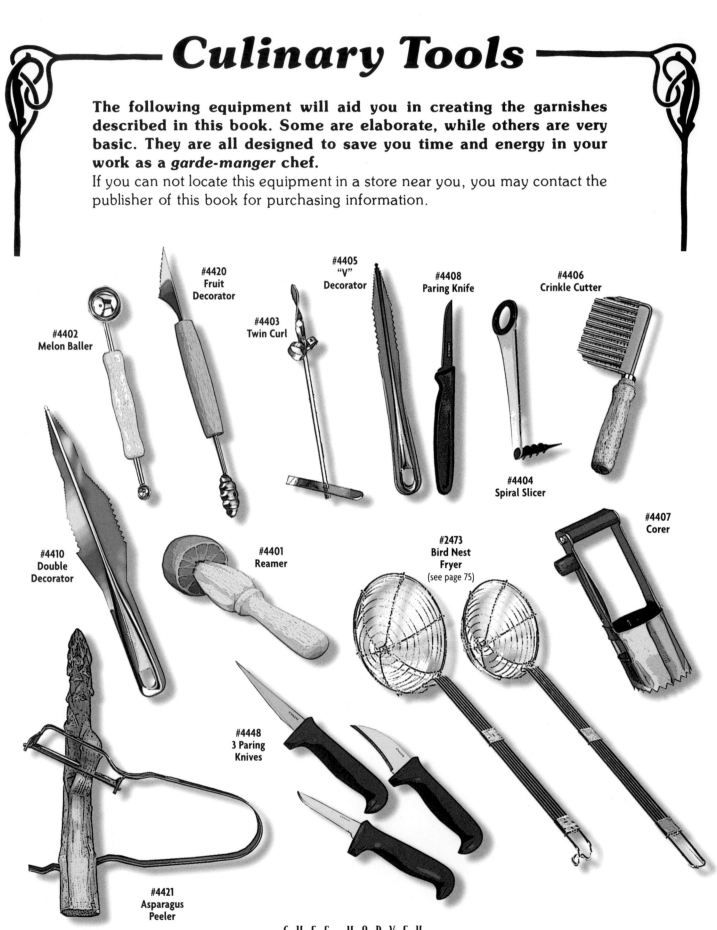

#4402
Melon Baller

#4420
Fruit
Decorator

#4403
Twin Curl

#4405
"V"
Decorator

#4408
Paring Knife

#4406
Crinkle Cutter

#4404
Spiral Slicer

#4410
Double
Decorator

#4401
Reamer

#2473
Bird Nest
Fryer
(see page 75)

#4407
Corer

#4448
3 Paring
Knives

#4421
Asparagus
Peeler

CHEF HARVEY

Paring Knife

Bird's Beak Knife

Parmesan Cheese Knife

Pointed Knife

Saw Knife

Utility Knife

Vegetable Knife

Mini Santoku Knife

#4481 8-Piece Knife Set

#4434
Melon Garnishing Book

#4479
Culinary Carving and Plate Decorating Book

#4503
Culinary Carving Video

Culinary Carving & Plate Decorations©
• Carrot Flower & Cucumber Arrangement
• Double Happiness Template
• Yellow Rose
• Tomato Arrangement
• Watermelon Rind Design
• Watermelon Dragon
• Carrot Cosmos
• Carnation
• Cranes Mean Longevity
• Dragons Dictate Fortune
• Melon Design
• Together Forever
• Orange Design
International Culinary Consultants
Web Site: www.chefharvey.com
#4503

#4424
Waffle Cutter

#4416
6-Piece Carving Set

#4425
Fruit-K-Bob® with Book

#4428
Pickle Slicer

#4417
Square Egg Mold
(see page 57)

"makes a square egg"

#4423
Grater

HOW TO GARNISH

Culinary Tools

#4480
80-Piece
Carving Set

#4422
22-Piece
Carving Set

#4451
Groovy
Groover

#SP101
Swiss
Peeler

#4449
Carrot
Curler

#4488
8-Piece
Melon Scoop
Set

#4489
6-Piece
Decorating
Set

#4482
Corrugated
Carving Set

#2416
Rex Slicer

CHEF HARVEY

14

#4504
How to Garnish DVD
(English & Spanish)

#4441
How to Garnish Book (Spanish)
with Culinary Tool Set

#4440
How to Garnish Book (Spanish)

#4431
How to Garnish Book (English)
with Culinary Tool Set

#4433
How to Garnish Book (English)

#4439
How to Garnish Book (French)
with Culinary Tool Set

#4438
How to Garnish Book (French)

#4502
How to Garnish
Video (Spanish)

#4501
How to Garnish
Video (English)

Design Cutters

These Unique Long Life Design Cutters Are
Hand Crafted From Heavy Gauge Stainless Steel

#4450-01
#4450-04
#4450-07
#4450-10
#4450-02
#4450-05
#4450-08
#4450-11
#4450-03
#4450-06
#4450-09
#4450-12
#4450-13

#4450-01 Turtle
#4450-02 Lobster
#4450-03 Butterfly

#4450-04 Dragon
#4450-05 Crab
#4450-06 Bird

#4450-07 Parrot
#4450-08 Goldfish
#4450-09 Fish

#4450-10 Tulip
#4450-11 Flower
#4450-12 Dragon (Large)
#4450-13 Phoenix

Apple Bird

Beautiful is the only word to describe this garnish

For the best results choose an apple that is well rounded, without blemishes or bruises.

A sharp serrated steak knife is recommended for cutting.

Cut off ⅓ from the side of an apple to provide a flat base.

This section will be used later to make the head and neck.

Place the apple before you cut side down with the stem facing you.

Use a light sawing motion to make a small wedge shaped cut at the top.

Continue making wedge shaped cuts each a bit larger than the previous one.

Repeat this on both sides, forming three sets of feathers.

If a piece breaks, do not worry, the sections will fit together and the break will not be noticeable.

Starting with the largest cut overlap consecutive smaller cuts.

The natural juices of the apple hold the feathers together.

To form the head and neck cut a ¼ inch slice from the center of the section set aside in the first step.

Cut a v at the front.

Leave some fruit at the front and then cut the fruit away for the neck following the contour of the skin.

Cloves or appleseeds may be used to make eyes.

Insert a toothpick into the body on an angle and attach the head and neck.

Prevent darkening by squeezing lemon juice over the entire surface of the apple bird.

To present the apple bird, use a potato for a base, cover it with greens and insert two toothpicks into the top.

Attach the bird in a dive bomb position and display.

See Photo Page 38 and 45

Apple Cup

The apple-of-your-eye becomes a unique container in no time at all.

Cut a slice from the bottom of a large, firm apple and stand it up.

Use a corregated garnishing tool to trim the outside of the apple.

Cut a slice from the top of the apple to make the cover of the cup.

Hollow the inside of the trimmed apple with a melon baller and fill with apple sauce, preserves or jelly.

See Photo Page 42

Red Cabbage Flower

This garnish is simple to make, beautiful and will be the center of conversation at your dining table.

Make cuts into a red cabbage half way in and ¾ of the way to the root.

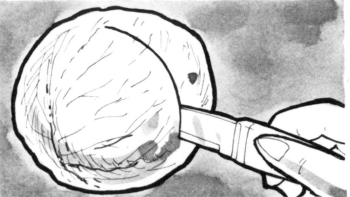

Continue making these cuts evenly around the cabbage.

Separate the layers and open up the flower.

See Photo Page 47

Canape Hors d'oeuvres

You'll hold the winning hand at your next card party when you serve these delightful treats.

Small bite-size sandwiches can be made in the shapes of hearts, diamonds, clubs and spades with the aid of canape cutters.

Place slices of different cold cuts, cheeses and breads before you on a cutting board.

Press the cutting edge of the cutter down through the food.
Repeat this, alternating bread, cheese and meat as desired.

When the canape cutter is filled, insert a toothpick through the center of sandwich and press the plunger to remove the hors d'oeuvre.

See Photo Page 39

HOW TO GARNISH

Carrot Blossoms

This floral garnish can be made from turnips as well as carrots.

Make long, thin, lengthwise slices from a large thick carrot or turnip.

Shape the slices into rectangles. Cut through the slices approximately 1/8 inch apart leaving about 1/2 inch on the edges.

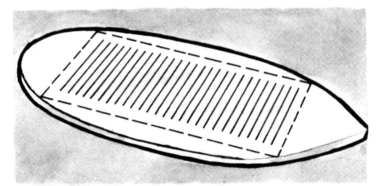

Soak in salt water until pliable.
Fold the slices in half lengthwise and roll them.
Secure at the bottom with a rubber band or floral tape.
Soak in ice water.

The petals may be left looped or can be cut for a variation.

CHEF HARVEY

Carrot Curls

Carrot curls add color to cold cut platters and salads.

Select a medium sized carrot at room temperature.

Use a vegetable peeler or a sharp paring knife to make thin length-wise carrot slices.

Curl each slice with your finger and fasten it with a toothpick.

Place in ice water.

When ready to use, remove toothpick.

See Photo Page 46

Sugar 'n Spice Grapes

In a small bowl beat an egg white until foamy.

Immerse a cluster of grapes into the egg white.

Shake off the excess egg white and sprinkle the grapes with a mixture of cinnamon and granulated or powdered sugar.

Place the grapes on wax paper and refrigerate them overnight.

See Photo Page 43

Carrot Flowers

This garnish can be made not only with carrots but also with cucumbers, beets, turnips, and potatoes. (Potatoes should be deep fat fried.)

Trim off both ends of a carrot. Score the outside with a corrugated garnishing tool.

Use a knife to slice the flowers to the desired thickness.

Carrot flowers can be used for salads or for cooking.

CARROT FLOWER VARIATION

Peel a large carrot.
Make three cuts slanted towards the center. (Be careful not to cut all of the way through the carrot.)

Carefully remove the newly formed flower.

Additional flowers are made by repeating the process.

Place an olive in the center of the carrot flower to complete the garnish.

Knots of Carrots

Tie your cold-cut platters together with a border of these easy-to-make carrot knots.

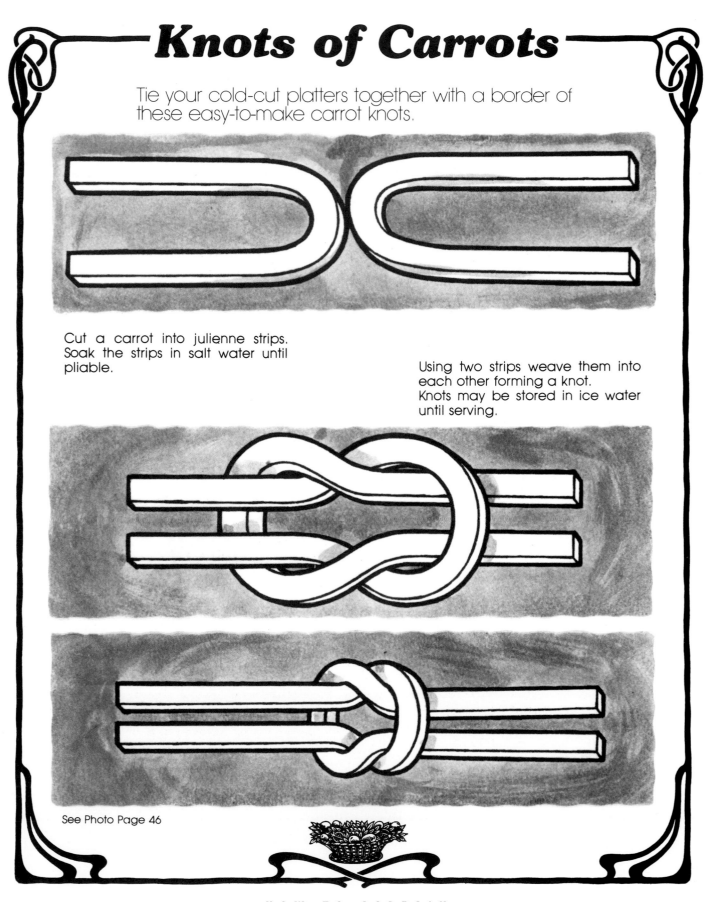

Cut a carrot into julienne strips. Soak the strips in salt water until pliable.

Using two strips weave them into each other forming a knot. Knots may be stored in ice water until serving.

See Photo Page 46

HOW TO GARNISH

Carrot Palm Tree

Bring a touch of the tropics to your table with this decorative garnish.

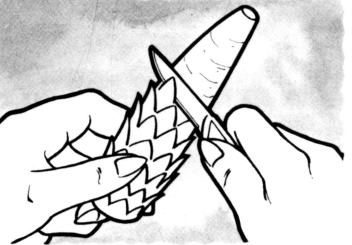

Peel a large thick carrot and cut off the very bottom and top.
Use a sharp knife to make small cuts into the carrot as shown.
Start at the bottom and encircle the carrot.

Alternate the cuts on each row.

Continue making these cuts to the top of the carrot.

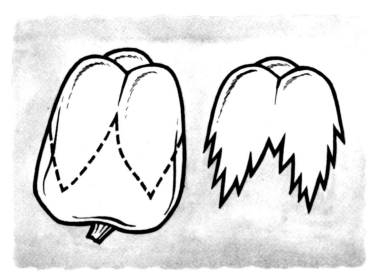

Select a green pepper with three "lobes" and cut the bottom of each lobe into ovals.

Core the pepper.
Jagged edges may be added to make the leaves.

Insert a toothpick into the top of the carrot and attach the pepper.
A potato may be used as a base by cutting a slice from the bottom to stabilize it and attaching the carrot with a few toothpicks.

Add greens around the base of the carrot to add color to the garnish.

See Photo Front Cover

Celery Flower

Instead of discarding the root end of a bunch of celery, use it to make a beautiful flower garnish.

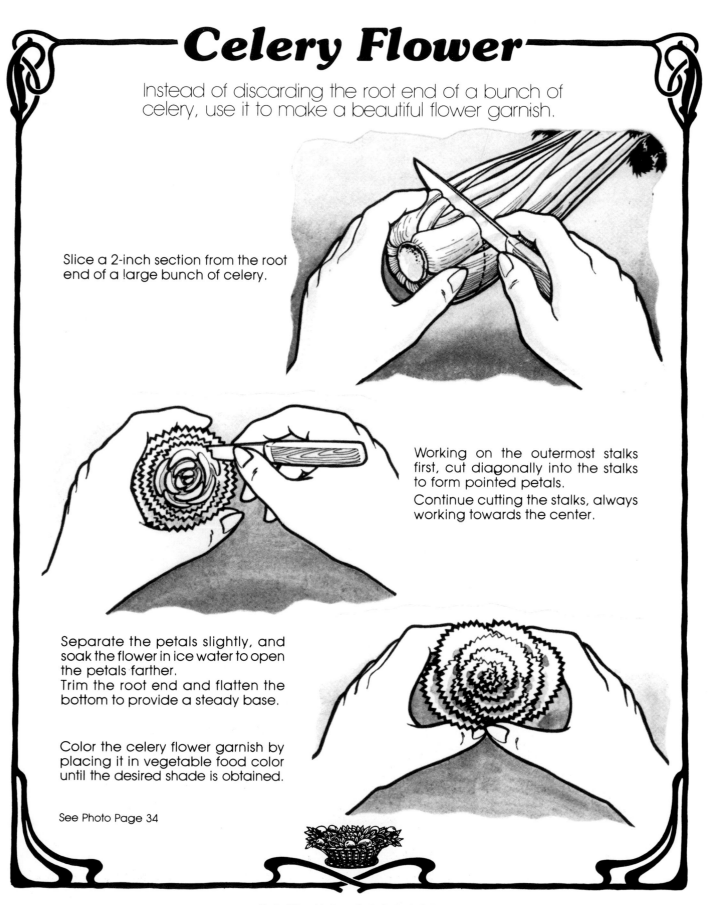

Slice a 2-inch section from the root end of a large bunch of celery.

Working on the outermost stalks first, cut diagonally into the stalks to form pointed petals.
Continue cutting the stalks, always working towards the center.

Separate the petals slightly, and soak the flower in ice water to open the petals farther.
Trim the root end and flatten the bottom to provide a steady base.

Color the celery flower garnish by placing it in vegetable food color until the desired shade is obtained.

See Photo Page 34

Stuffed Celery

A new treat for an old favorite vegetable.

Wash and trim the ends of the celery stalks.

Fill the center of the stalks with peanut butter, chopped liver, or cream cheese.

Two stalks may be put together to form a cylinder.

Hold them together with rubber bands until they stick.

Refrigerate until ready to use.

Cut the stuffed celery into bite-sized sections and serve.

Citrus Cartwheels

Select a citrus fruit with a thick rind for the best results.

Use the eye opening of a food decorating tool or a zester to make orange, lemon, or lime cartwheels.

Push the eye opening of the tool into the skin at the blossom end and pull down all the way to the other end.
Do this in an even pattern around the entire fruit.

Slice the fruit and remove the seeds.

Cartwheels can be used to decorate watermelon baskets, mixed drinks or punch.

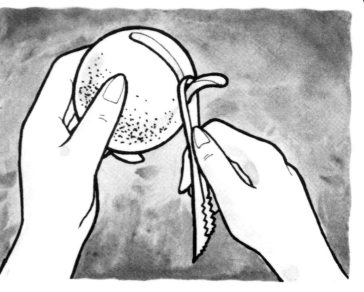

See Photo Page 37

HOW TO GARNISH

Citrus Elephant

Your guests will never forget this delightful pachyderm.

This garnish can be made from any citrus fruit: lemons, limes, oranges, or grapefruits.

To make the tail cut a V just above the stem end of the fruit.

Carve a Y at the other end to make the trunk.
Use a knife to raise the skin from the fruit without detaching it.

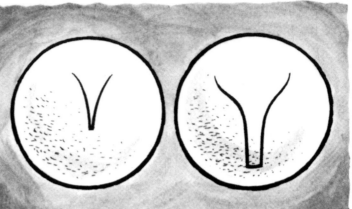

The ears of the elephant are made by making partial slices on the sides of the fruit towards the trunk end.

Pull the skin away from the fruit without pulling it off.

Attach gumdrops or marshmallows with toothpicks to make the feet and eyes.

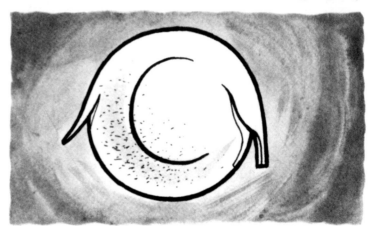

See Photo Page 42

CHEF HARVEY

28

Citrus Gelatin Wedges

This colorful easy-to-make treat will become a
delight not only for your guests but for you as well.

For the best results choose a thick-
skinned citrus fruit for this garnish.
Cut the desired citrus fruit in half.

Remove the pulp, without breaking
the skin, to form a shell.

Prepare a flavored gelatin as in-
structed on the package.
Fill each shell with the gelatin mixture and chill until firm.

Use a heated knife to cut into
wedges.

See Photo Page 42

HOW TO GARNISH

Citrus Strip Rose

This garnish can easily be made from any citrus fruits including oranges, lemons, or grapefruits.

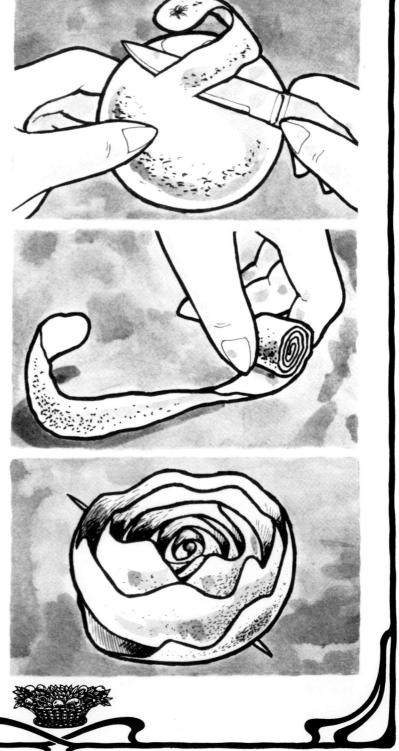

With a sharp paring knife peel the skin from the citrus fruit.
Start at the stem end and peel the skin in a continuous strip ¾ inch wide.
Remove the pulp from the skin.

Form the rose by rolling the skin in a tight coil keeping the stem end to the outside.

Hold the rose together with a toothpick.

See Photo Page 46

Centipede Slice

This cute little critter will brighten up your table and bring smiles to your guests' faces.

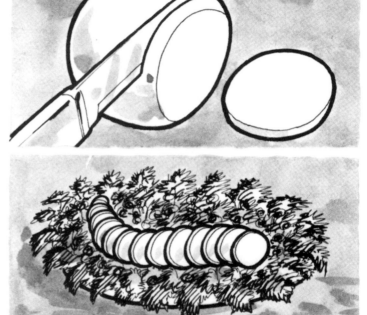

Cut a carrot, radish, tomato or cucumber into thin slices.

Arrange these slices according to size.

Half of a cherry tomato may be used as a head, cloves or bits of carrots as eyes and pipe cleaners or tooth-picks as antennae.

See Photo Page 35

Cucumber Crab

This crab is no grouch and makes everyone smile when displayed on your table.

Cut off the ends of the cucumber.

Cut the cucumber in half length-wise.

Two crabs can be made from the same cucumber.

Cut four thin, parallel slices on both ends, making sure not to go completely through.

To form legs, make a slice on each side and cut out a section from the center.

Carve v's at the end of the legs to form claws.

Soak in salt water until pliable.
Bend every other thin slice into a loop.
Soak in cold water.
Insert match sticks as eyes.

See Photo Page 45

CHEF HARVEY

32

Party Basket

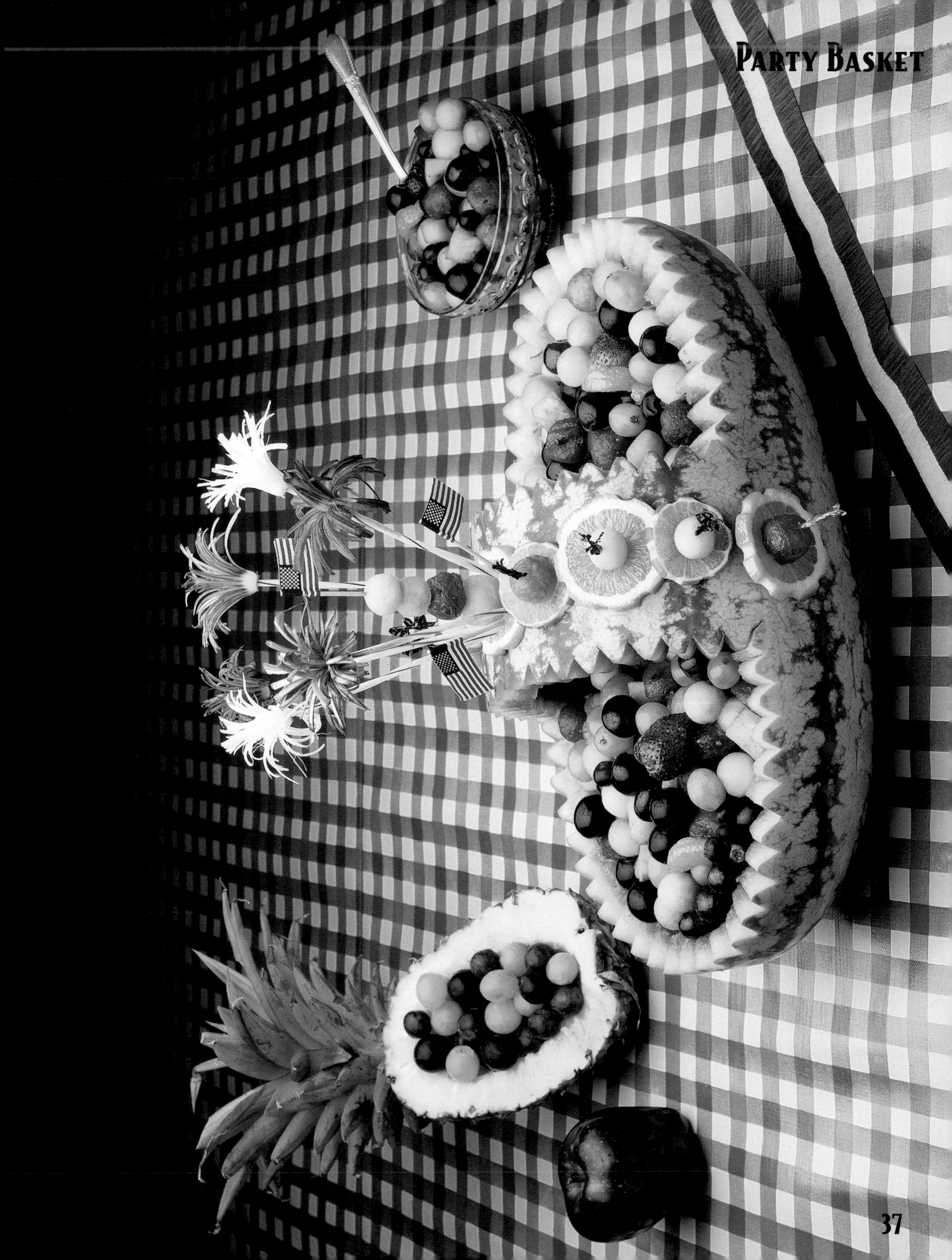

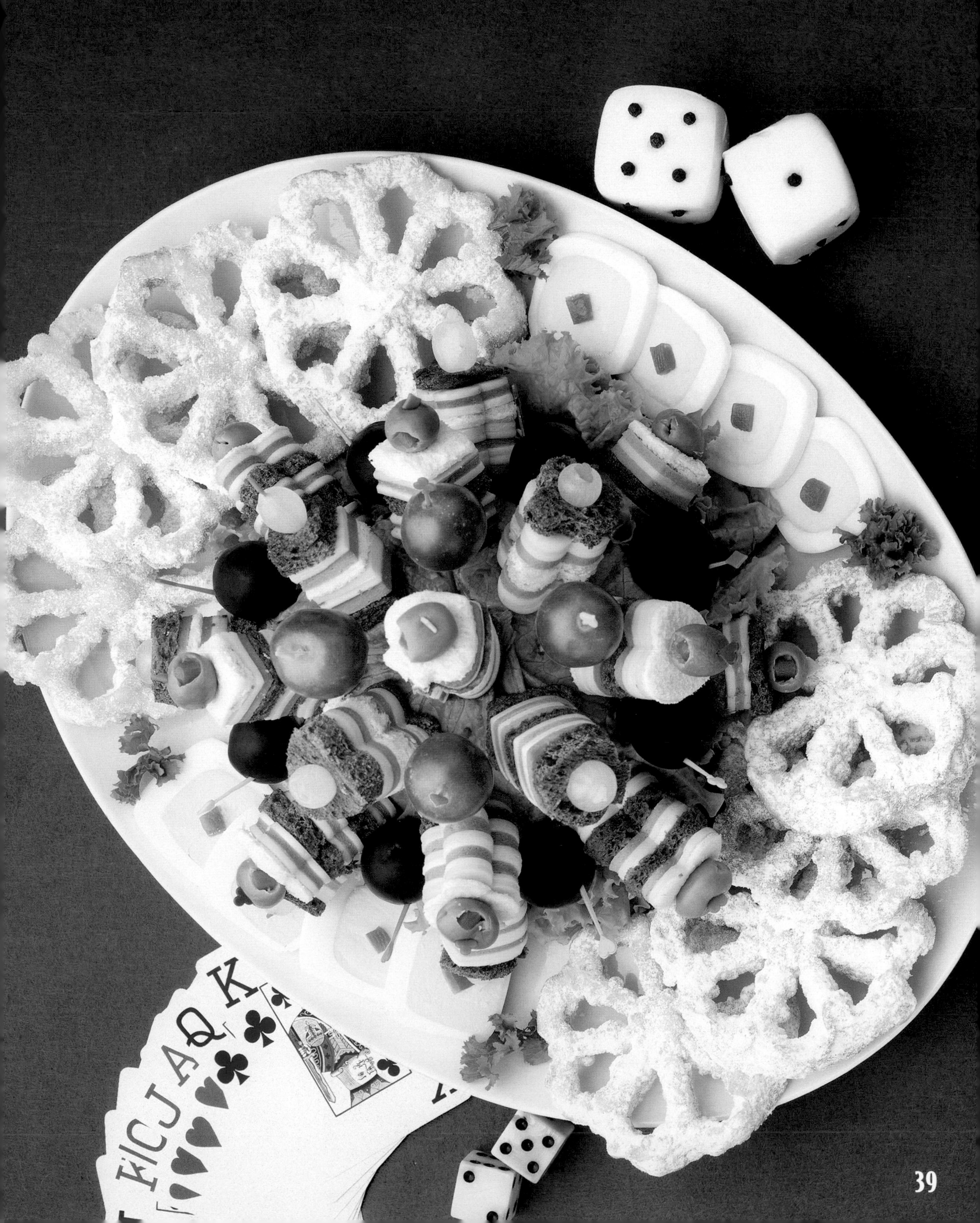

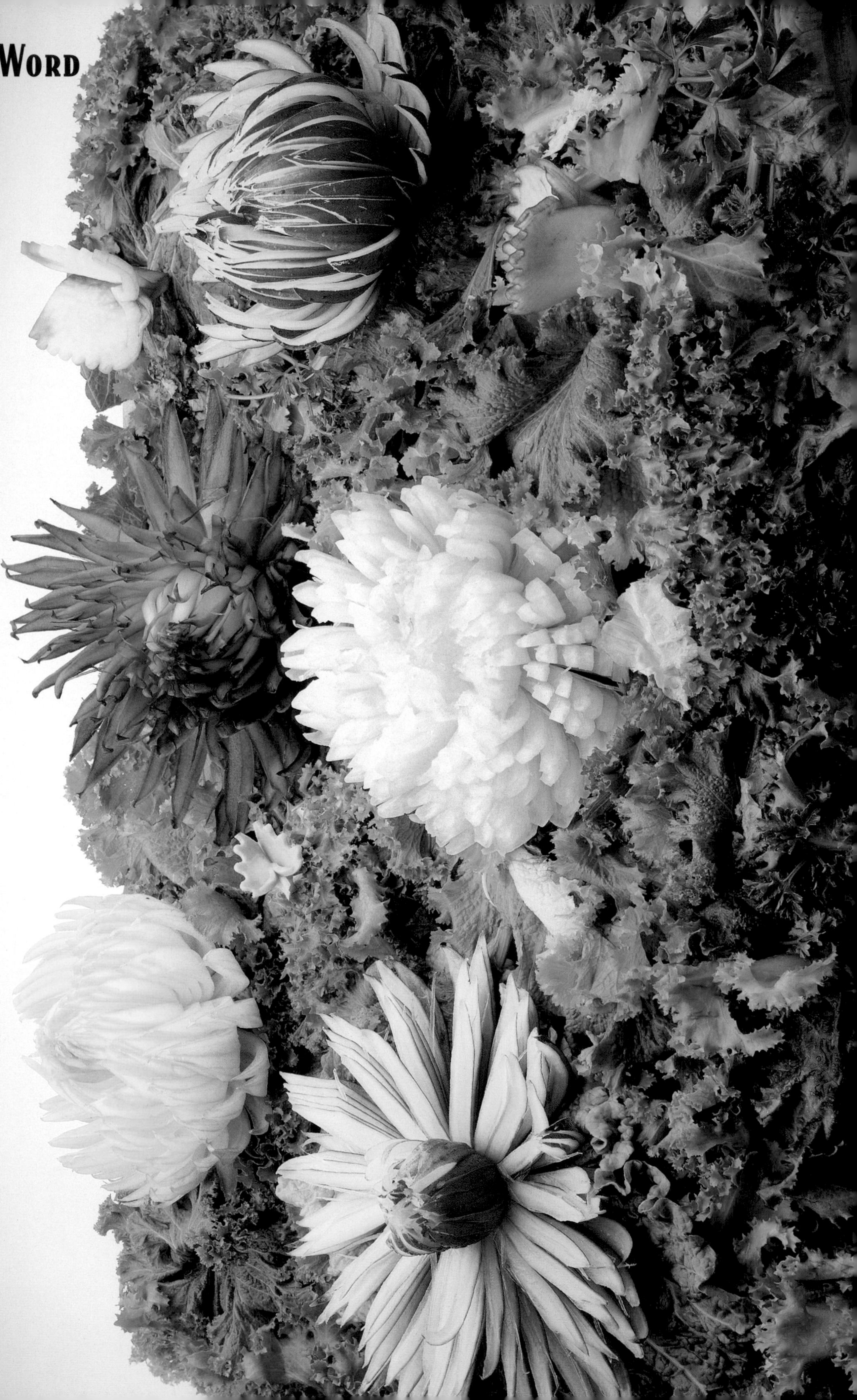

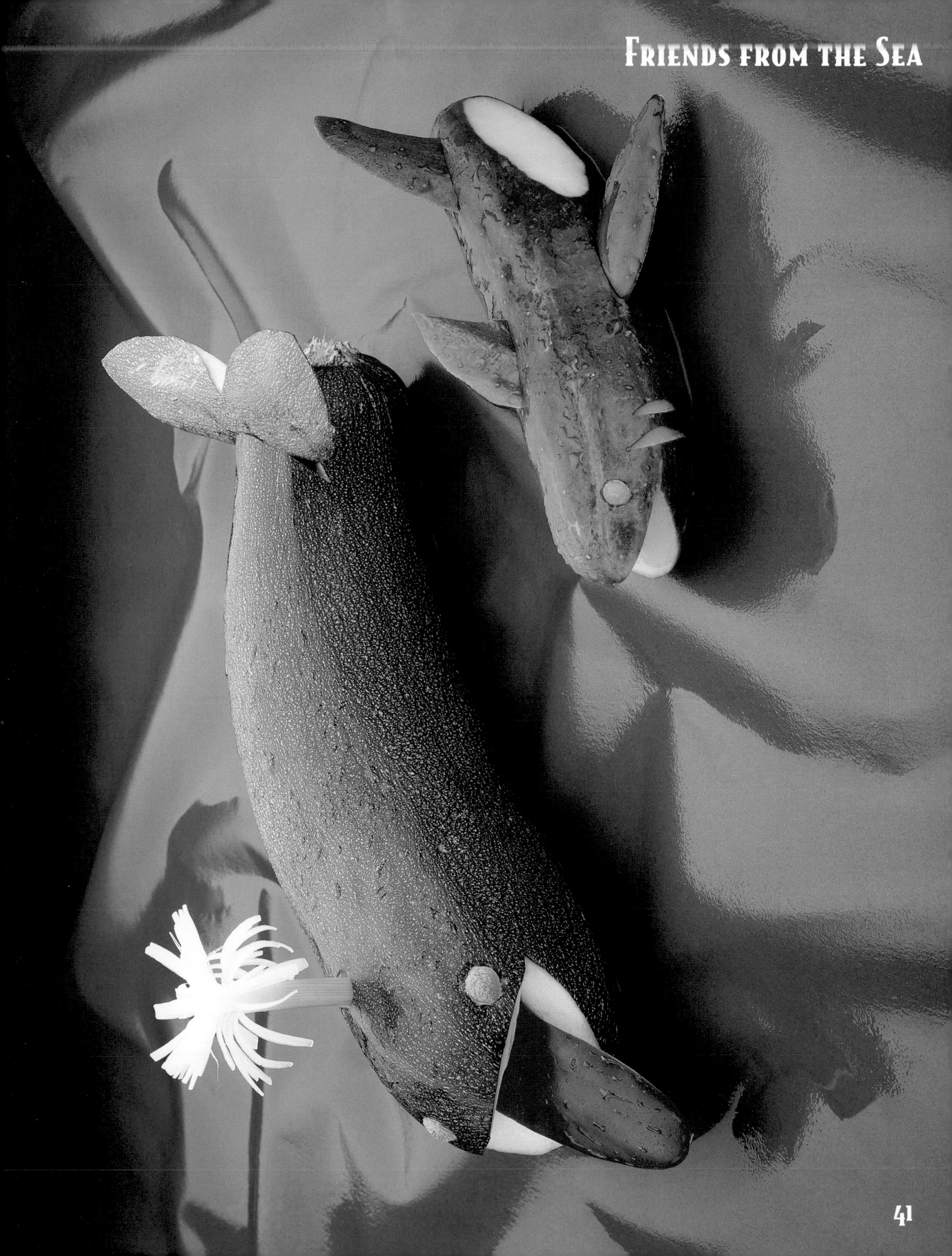

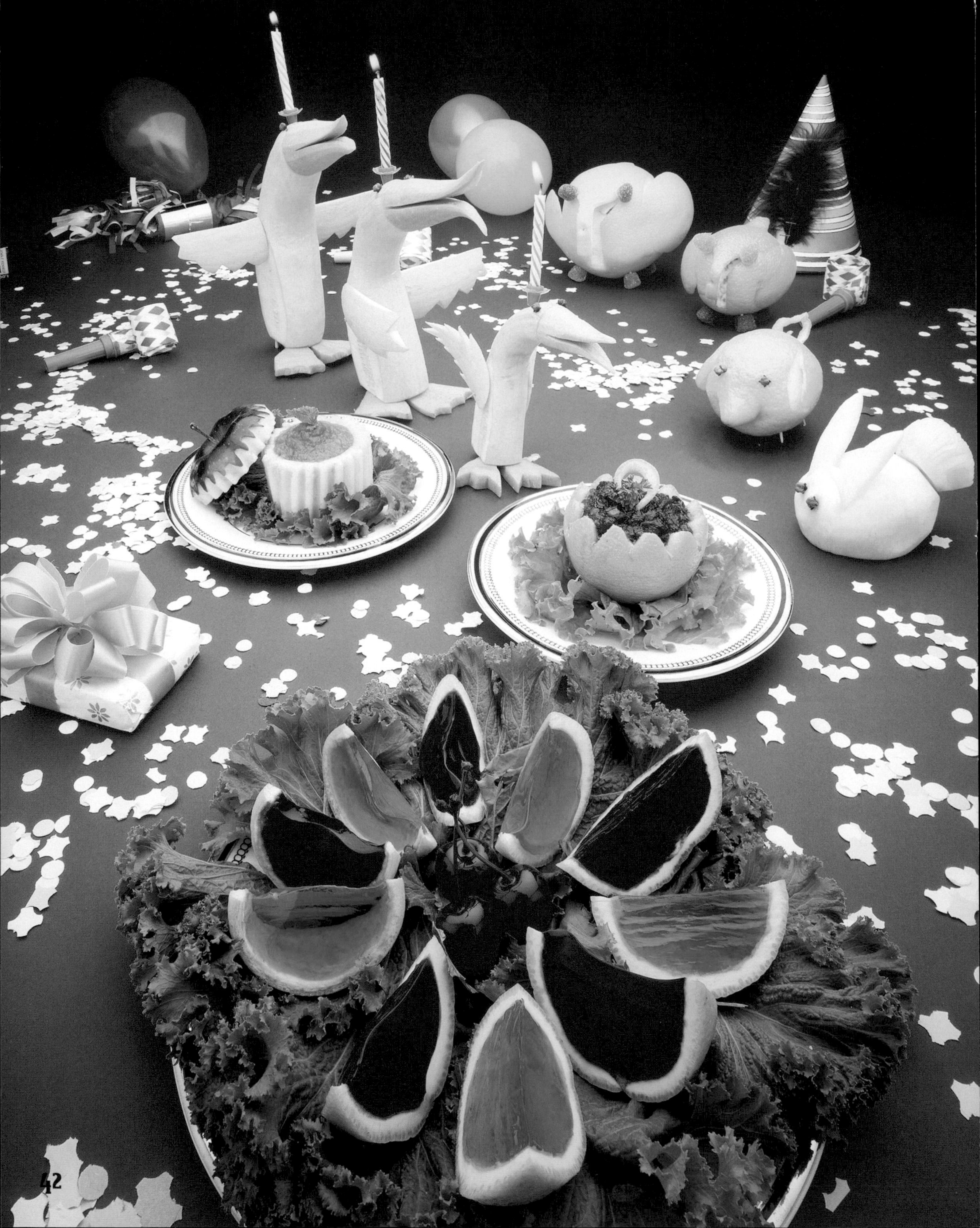

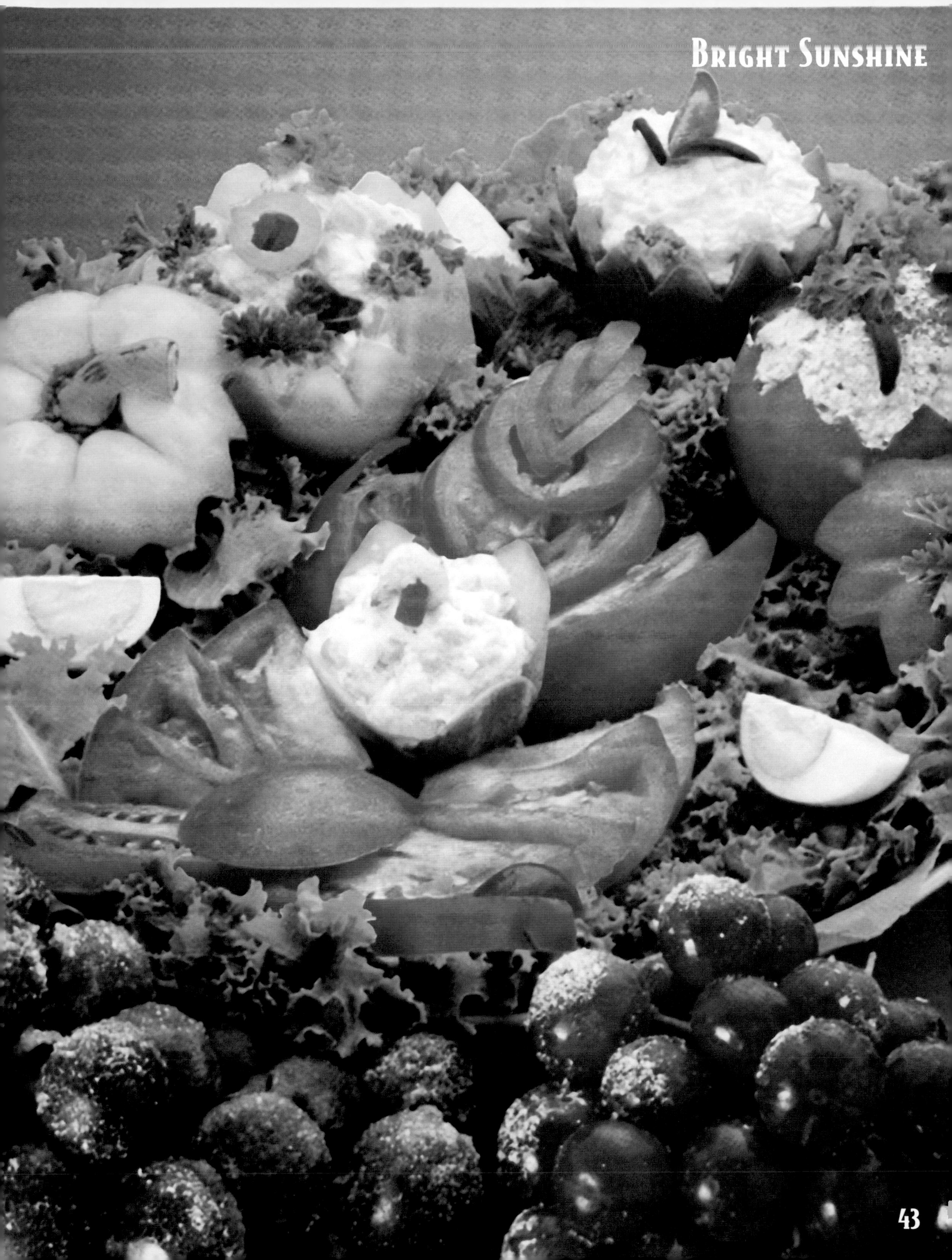

VEGETABLE TWIST

SILLY GOOSE

ONION MUM

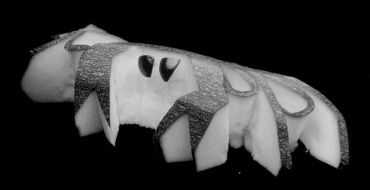

CUCUMBER CRAB

APPLE BIRD

SUNNY BLOSSOM

Delightful Surprise

46

Butternut Squash Centerpiece

The butternut squash centerpiece is an attractive, inexpensive garnish that is easy to make.

Select a uniformly shaped, firm eggplant or butternut squash for the vase of the centerpiece.

Cut a slice from the top and another from the bottom to provide a stable base.

To decorate the vase, carve or use a cookie cutter to shape turnip, carrot, or eggplant slices into a flower shape.

Secure the flower to the vase by means of a toothpick.

Attach a small piece of carrot to the end of the toothpick.

Large scallions are used to make the flowers and background foliage.

Cut the scallion approximately 2 inches from the root end.

To make the background, cut the ends of the greens on an angle and attach them to the vase with a toothpick or skewer.

Baby's breath, pussy willows or other decorations may be added to enhance the background.

The flowers are made from the onion portion.

Cut off the roots but leave the root end intact.

Make slices into the center and across the vegetable.

Continue making these slices around the entire onion, keeping them as close together as possible.

Insert a toothpick into the root end and spin the onion to separate the petals.

The odor of the onion may be removed by soaking it in hot water with lemon.

Soak in ice water.

Decorate the flower by dipping it in food coloring.

Spin off the excess in the sink and attach the flower to the background with the toothpick.

See Photo Page 48

Cucumber Rose

A rose by any other name could be a cucumber.

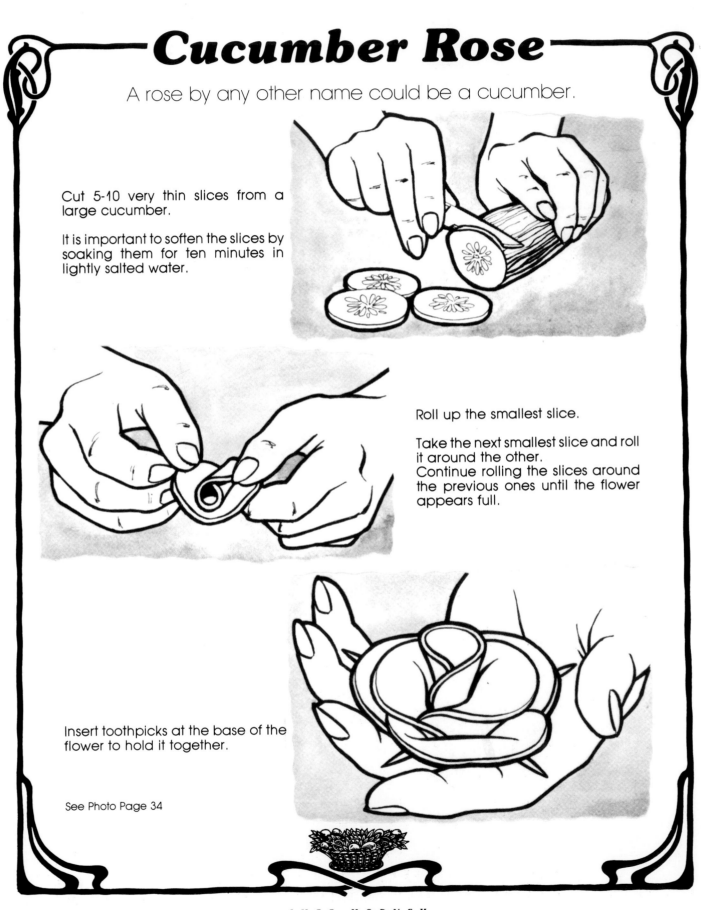

Cut 5-10 very thin slices from a large cucumber.

It is important to soften the slices by soaking them for ten minutes in lightly salted water.

Roll up the smallest slice.

Take the next smallest slice and roll it around the other.
Continue rolling the slices around the previous ones until the flower appears full.

Insert toothpicks at the base of the flower to hold it together.

See Photo Page 34

CHEF HARVEY

50

Scored Cucumber

The popular cucumber changes its shape and
taste appeal with a few simple cuts.

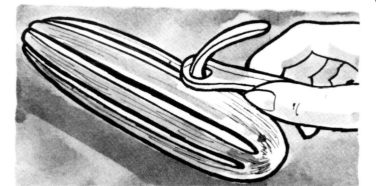

Evenly score the outside of a
cucumber with a zester or a corrugated garnishing tool.

Cut into slices.

See Photo Page 46

Cucumber Chain

Cut a scored cucumber in half.
Hollow the center of each half to
form a tubular shell by using a twin
curl cutter or a melon baller.
Cut into ¼ inch slices.

Cut a slice in every other slice and
link the slices together to form a
chain.

See Photo Page 46

Cucumber Shark

The "villain of the sea" is now everyone's friend when he decorates your table.

For the best results select a cucumber that is slightly curved.

Slice a quarter inch off the bottom of the cucumber.
This piece is used later to make the top fins.
Cut a wedge out of the front of the cucumber to form the mouth.
Cut two smaller wedges on each side just behind the mouth to form the gills.
Hollow out two holes for the eyes.

Approximately two-thirds of the way back carve out a ¼ inch slice from each side of the cucumber to make the side fins.

Using the piece from the bottom of the cucumber, make the top fins by cutting it in half diagonally.

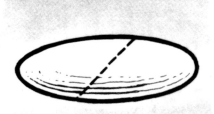

Carve out two slots in the top of the cucumber, one behind the other and insert the top fins.

Carve out two slots on each side of the cucumber, and insert the side fins.

See Photo Front Cover and Page 41

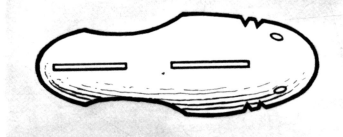

Cucumber Shrimp Boat

Guests will dock at your table when the cucumber shrimp boat sails into view.

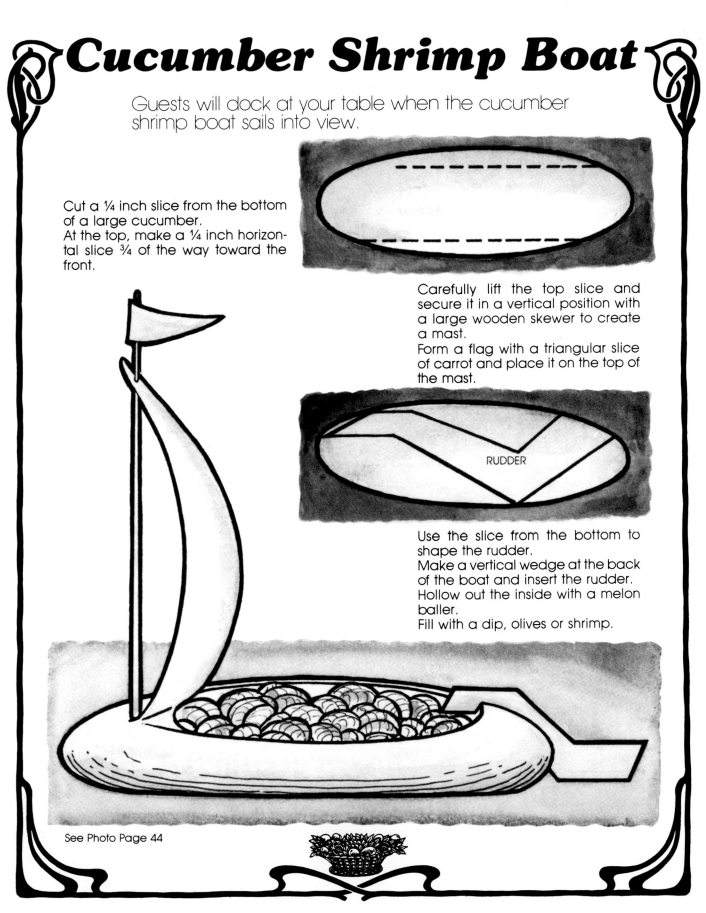

Cut a ¼ inch slice from the bottom of a large cucumber.
At the top, make a ¼ inch horizontal slice ¾ of the way toward the front.

Carefully lift the top slice and secure it in a vertical position with a large wooden skewer to create a mast.
Form a flag with a triangular slice of carrot and place it on the top of the mast.

RUDDER

Use the slice from the bottom to shape the rudder.
Make a vertical wedge at the back of the boat and insert the rudder.
Hollow out the inside with a melon baller.
Fill with a dip, olives or shrimp.

See Photo Page 44

Cucumber Stairs

Create a puzzling and attractive garnish with a few simple cuts

Score a 3 inch section of cucumber with a corrugated garnishing tool.

Insert a knife into the center of the section.

On each side of the cucumber, make opposite diagonal crinkle cuts using the corrugated garnishing tool.

Store in ice water until ready to serve.

See Photo Page 34

Stuffed Cucumbers

A cucumber becomes a holder for your favorite filling with this easy to make garnish.

Cut a large cucumber in half and work on each half separately.

The skin of the cucumber may be scored if desired.

Hollow the soft center of the cucumber with an apple corer or a twin curl cutter.

Insert the point of the twin curl and attach the key to the end of the shaft.

Press lightly and turn the tool clockwise, removing the soft section as you go.

Be sure to pierce the end of the cucumber.

Stuff the hollow shell with mixtures of chopped pickle, salmon or chives with cream cheese.

Place in the refrigerator until firm and then cut into slices.

The cucumber shell can also be stuffed with a carrot and cut into slices.

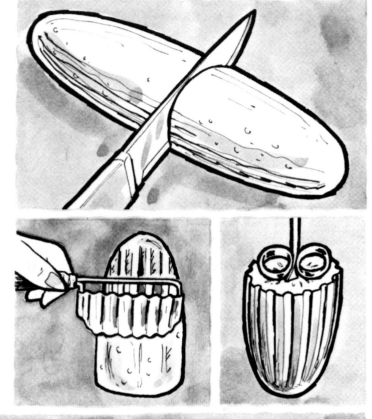

See Photo Page 38

Eggplant Sunflower

A pleasure to make, a delight to the eye and a beautiful center-piece for your table.

Cut off the bottom and top of a small firm eggplant.

With a sharp paring knife score the outer skin ⅔ of the way to the bottom forming eight equal sections.

Give each section a pointed petal shape.

Peel the skin away from the meat of the vegetable.
Remove the meat from the center.
Score the center and decorate with food coloring.

To prevent darkening coat the garnish with a mixture of lemon juice and water.

CHEF HARVEY

Square Eggs

Turns hard boiled eggs into a unique taste treat.

Place a warm peeled egg into the egg press.

Put the pressing plate on top of the egg.
Screw the top on until the egg becomes square.

Chill the egg press in a refrigerator for 5 to 10 minutes.
Unscrew the top and push the bottom plate up to remove the square egg.

Add cloves to form a pair of dice or cut into slices to form unique square egg pieces.
Perfect for salads, snacks or hors d'oeuvres.

See Photo Page 39

Fancy Edges

Make fancy edges on oranges, lemons, grapefruits and melons to add a festive flair to your table.

Create this garnish by using a sharp paring knife if a v-shaped food decorator is not available. Insert the point of the v-shaped decorator into the fruit.

Make each v cut next to the one before it, being sure they connect.

Go all the way around the fruit. Separate the two sections.

See Photo Page 33

CHEF HARVEY

Leek Flower

The lowly leek blossoms into a beautiful flower with a few simple cuts.

Remove the roots but do not remove the root end, and trim off the green section of the leek.

Starting ½ of an inch from the root end make parallel slices into the center and across the length of the vegetable.

Continue to make these slices close together and continue around the entire vegetable.

Separate the petals carefully by hand.

Use a melon baller to shape a carrot ball.

Push a wooden skewer through the root end of the leek and attach the carrot ball to the end.

To give the garnish a professional look, dip the edges of the flower in food coloring.

See Photo Page 45

Leek Ribbons

Easy to make and pleasing to the eye, this garnish will fascinate your guests.

Trim away the roots and green section from a large leek.

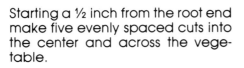

Starting a ½ inch from the root end make five evenly spaced cuts into the center and across the vegetable.

Soak in warm water until each section is pliable.

Tuck the outer layer towards the center.

Continue to do this for each inner layer until you reach the top. Soak in ice water.

The appearance of the leek ribbon can be enhanced by tinting it with food coloring.

Lemon Curl

Add a little zest to your meals with these mighty mini lemon garnishes.

Cut a lemon into quarters.

Use a paring knife to peel the outer rind ¾ of the way back.

Curl the rind back and attach with a toothpick.

See Photo Page 44

Lemon Outrigger

Cut a lemon into quarters.

Attach two toothpicks to a carrot stick and attach to the lemon wedge.

See Photo Front Cover

Lemon Pig

There's nothing fishy about "this little piggy"...he's the perfect garnish for any seafood platter.

For best results choose a lemon with a pointed end.
Make a horizontal cut across the center of the point to form the mouth.

Form the ears by making diagonal cuts on both sides ⅓ of the way beginning from the pointed end.
Create the curly tail by means of a zester or a sharp paring knife.
Use cloves for eyes and toothpicks for legs.

See Photo Page 42

CHEF HARVEY

Melon Basket

Melon sculptures can be created easily with the help of a v-shaped food decorating tool.

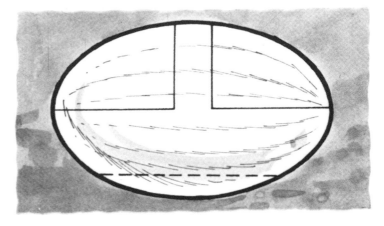

For the best results, select a melon that is oval in shape.

To provide a stable base, cut a thin slice from the bottom of the melon.

Draw the lines of the basket on the melon before you start cutting.

Draw one line horizontally around the center of the melon.

Then draw the handle by drawing two lines a few inches apart at the top of the melon.

Cut an X through the rind in the sections to be discarded to reduce the chances of splitting.

Use a v-shaped food decorating tool to make the zig zag pattern along the edges.

Insert the point of the tool at least half way into the melon along the line that was just drawn.

Continue making v-shaped cuts along the line being sure they connect.

Be careful not to cut through the handle.

When the cutting is completed, lift the top quarter sections off carefully.

Use a knife to remove the pulp of the watermelon from the rind.

A melon ball scoop may be used to form balls to fill the basket.

Also, fruits such as grapes, cherries, strawberries, pineapple, and various melons may be used to fill the melon, if desired.

Decorate the handle with citrus slices, melon balls, and cherries attached with toothpicks to give the basket a professional touch.

See Photo Page 37

Melon Buggy

The perfect centerpiece for that special baby shower or party.

Slice a thin section from the bottom of the melon to provide a stable base and draw the pattern as shown.

Use a sharp knife to cut out the section which is used to make the buggy's handle.

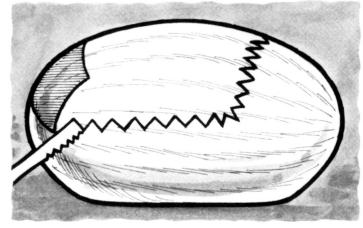

To make the handle, use a knife and cut the end section as shown and remove the pulp from the rind. Use a v-shaped food decorating tool to make the zig zag edge along the side.

Remove the top section of the rind and hollow out the inside.
Use this to make melon balls.
Attach the handle, skin up, with toothpicks.

Attach wheels made from citrus slices to the melon with toothpicks. Fill the shell with melon balls or fruit salad.

Melon Ship

Your table becomes an exciting port when the melon ship docks there.

Choose an elongated melon for this sculpture.
To stabilize the ship, cut a thin slice from the bottom of the melon.
Use a v-shaped food decorating tool like a pencil and draw the lines of the ship as shown.
Cut an x through the rind in the top of the melon to reduce the chances of splitting.

A v-shaped food decorating tool can be used to make the zig zag pattern along the lines just drawn. Be sure to insert the tool at least halfway into the melon.
Make cuts to form the front and back of the ship with a sharp knife. The cuts should all connect.

To aid in removing the rind, use a knife to make a deep cut in the top section and remove the section in two pieces.

Remove the pulp of the watermelon and fill the ship with the desired fruit.

To make the sails, cut sheets of stiff paper into the correct shape.
Attach the sails to the ship with a long skewer.

Messages for any occasion can be written on the sails.

Melon Swan

This graceful melon swan adds a touch of elegance to even the simplest of meals.

The swan looks most attractive when it is made from a melon that is spherical in shape.

Cut a slice from the bottom of the melon to provide a stable base.

Draw the pattern for the swan as shown.

Use a sharp knife to cut along the lines drawn to form the head.

Be careful to leave the beak attached to the feathers.

A v-shaped food decorating tool may be used to shape the feathers.

Use a knife to hollow out an eye.

Do not attempt to remove the top section in one piece.

Cut it into quarters to aid in its removal.

Hollow the melon and trim the feathers so they are not too thick.

Use a melon ball scoop to form balls from the removed melon.

Fill the swan with strawberries, raspberries, blueberries, grapes, cherries, melon balls or any other mixed fruit.

See Photo Page 33

CHEF HARVEY

66

Melon Whale

This whimsical whale holds cool and colorful treats.

An elongated melon should be used for the best results.

To stabilize the whale cut a thin slice from the bottom of the melon. Draw the lines of the whale as shown.

Cut an X through the rind in the section that is to be discarded. This will help prevent splitting of ripe watermelon.

Use a v-shaped food decorating tool to make the zig zag edges along the side.
Use a sharp paring knife to cut the tail and head section.

Cut the top section in quarters to aid in the removal of the rind.
Use a small paring knife to carve the mouth and eyes.

Hollow the shell and fill it with melon balls or mixed fruit.

See Photo Page 36

Olive-Scallion Pompom Flower

As a decorative border, circle your platters of cold cuts with these easy-to-make pompom flowers.

Slice off a 3-inch section from the stem of a small scallion.
Remove the root end.

The petals are made by slicing the scallion bulb into many thin slivers.
Spin the scallion to separate the petals.
Soak the scallion in ice water for 5-10 minutes to allow the ends to curl.

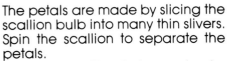

Color the scallion by placing it in vegetable food coloring.

Cut off the ends of a large pitted olive.
Push the scallion flower into the olive.

See Photo Page 46

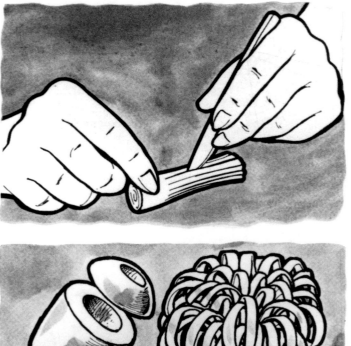

CHEF HARVEY

Onion Cup

In a matter of minutes you can turn an ordinary onion into a delightful serving cup.

Select a large round onion that does not have a double growth.

A white or red onion may be used.

Bermuda onions or red Spanish onions are more colorful.

The onion selected should not have soft spots, and the outer paper skin should be dry and not loose.

Use a V-shaped food decorating tool or a sharp paring knife to make a zig-zag cut around the "equator" of the onion.

Soak the two halves in hot water for a few minutes to remove the odor.

To separate the layers, remove the core of the onion by cutting a small circle around it and removing it with the point of a knife.

Push up the layers of onion with your thumb through the hole left by removing the core.

Each cup will be progressively smaller.

Use each cup to serve cooked vegetables such as peas, carrots or corn.

See Photo Page 47

Red Onion Flower

Turn a red onion into a flower with a few magical cuts.

Make three deep petal-shaped cuts around the side of a red onion.

Separate the individual petals.

Attach the ends of three equally sized petals with a toothpick.

Attach a carrot ball to the end of the toothpick and display.

Use the next set of equally sized petals to form the next flower.

Onion Mum

Mum's the word for this attractive onion garnish.

Select a large, tall, white or red onion for this garnish.
Try to select an onion with a single growth.

Use a paring knife to make cuts half way into the onion, 3/4 of the way to the root end.

Place a toothpick into the root end and immerse in hot water for a few minutes to remove the odor.
Then soak in ice water to open the petals further.

White onion mums can be colored with food coloring to enhance the appearance.

See Photo Page 40 and 45

HOW TO GARNISH

Orange Basket

Fun to make, easy to do and pretty to look at.

Cut a thin slice from the bottom of the orange to make a flat resting surface.
Use a zester or the eye opening of a food decorator to cut strips from the skin of the orange.
Start at the top and cut strips down towards the flat surface.
Stop before you reach the bottom.
Go all the way around the orange.

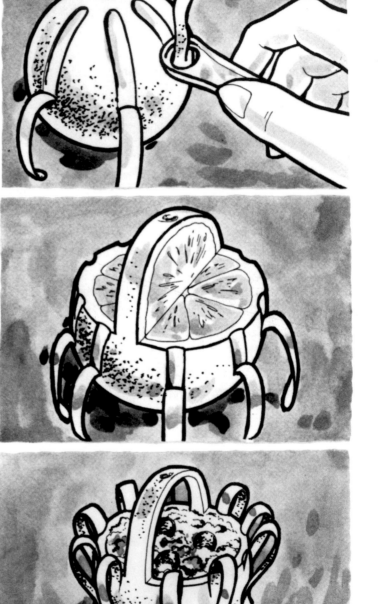

Cut away two wedges at the top of the orange.

Remove the pulp so you are left with a handle in the middle.

Fold over the strips to make loops. Remove the pulp from the orange and fill with cranberry sauce, apple sauce or fruit.

Pear Mouse

This whimsical guest is a pure delight for both children and adults.

Cut two lengthwise slices from the side of a pear.

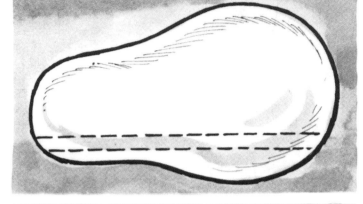

Use the inner slice to shape the ears.

Cut slits into the pear and attach the ears.

Use toothpicks as whiskers, cloves as eyes and a pipe cleaner as a tail.

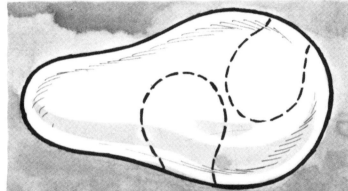

Red Pepper Flower

Add a touch of color and delicate beauty to your table with this red pepper flower.

Holding the stem end down cut v-shaped slices ¾ of the way down.

Carefully separate the seeds from the inside of the pepper wall.
Bend the petals outward.
Soak in cold water for five minutes.

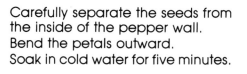

Potato Bird's Nest

Compliments will hatch a-plenty when this bird's nest is holding your favorite filling.

Shred, slice or julienne a peeled potato with a mandoline or a hand held slicer.

Mix in 1½ tablespoons of cornstarch.

Place two large handfulls of the potatoes in the larger basket.

Position the smaller basket over the potatoes in the larger basket.

Press down firmly and slide the clamp into place to secure the two baskets together.
Deep fry until the potatoes are golden brown.
Remove the clamp and the smaller basket.
Gently remove the nest from the larger basket.
Use the nest to present a bird garnish or to serve your favorite culinary delights: vegetables, eggs, chicken, etc.

See Photo Page 38

HOW TO GARNISH

Stuffed Potatoes

A new idea for everyone's favorite vegetable.

Use a twin curl cutter to hollow the center of a baking potato.
Insert the point of the tool into the end of the potato and attach the handle to the end of the shaft.
Press lightly and turn the tool clockwise.

When the double ring appears at the other end, remove the handle and slide the shaft through.

Remove the solid curls from the center by turning them clockwise. Stuff the hollowed potato shell with cheese, chopped meat, sausage or other food.

Wrap the potato in saran wrap for a microwave oven or aluminum foil for a conventional oven and bake.

STUFFED POTATO RECIPE
4 med. baking potatoes
1 egg
1 package onion soup mix
1 lb. chopped beef
3 tbsp. barbecue sauce

Bake the hollowed pototoes 10 minutes in a microwave oven on high or 45 minutes in a conventional oven at 350°F.
Let stand while preparing the following:
Beat the egg with a fork, add the package of onion soup mix, mix well; add the chopped beef and the barbecue sauce to the egg and soup mixture. Fill the pre-cooked potatoes with this filling and then micro-cook them another 5-8 minutes or bake them for another 15 minutes.

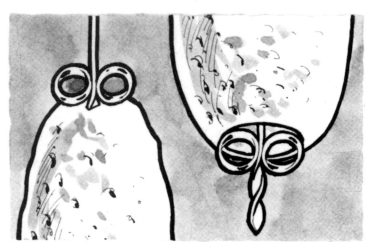

CHEF HARVEY

Radish Blossom

The radish blossom can make your meals bloom into something special.

While holding the radish with the stem end down, make a diagonal cut close to the bottom and less than half way into the radish.

Make the next cut above the previous cut leaving a thin petal. Continue making these petals along the entire length of the radish.

Turn the radish and make another set of petals on the opposite side. Place the blossom in ice water to open the petals and insert a toothpick at the base for a stem.

Radish Star

With a sharp paring knife, cut a v-shaped wedge at the top of the radish.
Cut two more v-shaped wedges to form a star.

To form petals on the side, make diagonal cuts into the radish.
Soak in ice water.

See Photo Page 46

Radish Flowers

A few simple cuts turn a ordinary radish into a beautiful flower.

Cut off the top of a large round radish.

Make diagonal cuts into the radish towards the bottom.

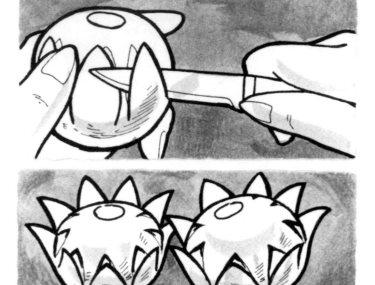

Peel the skin from the top and sides.

Place the flower in ice water to separate the petals.

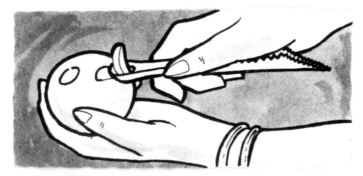

Radish Rose

Use the eye opening of a food decorator or a zester to make the petals of a rose.
Hold the radish with the root end up.

Start at the top and peel off the skin by pulling the tool down the side.
Stop before you get to the bottom.
Repeat this evenly around the radish.

Place the garnish in ice water and the petals will open up further.

See Photo Page 46

CHEF HARVEY

78

Radish Mushroom

A radish is a radish except when it's a mushroom.

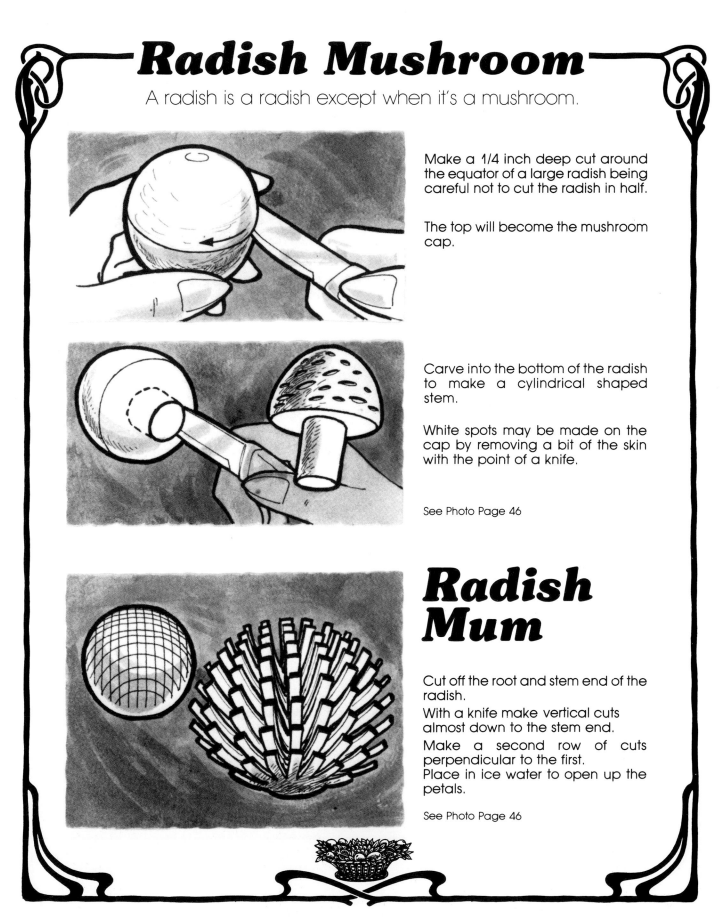

Make a 1/4 inch deep cut around the equator of a large radish being careful not to cut the radish in half.

The top will become the mushroom cap.

Carve into the bottom of the radish to make a cylindrical shaped stem.

White spots may be made on the cap by removing a bit of the skin with the point of a knife.

See Photo Page 46

Radish Mum

Cut off the root and stem end of the radish.

With a knife make vertical cuts almost down to the stem end.

Make a second row of cuts perpendicular to the first.

Place in ice water to open up the petals.

See Photo Page 46

Radish Propeller

A new twist to a common vegetable adds color and appeal to any meal.

Holding the root end down, cut into the top of the radish diagonally and carve down and to the side.

Make the cuts 3/4 of the way to the bottom.
Repeat to form three evenly spaced strips.

See Photo Page 46

Radish Fan

With an oval radish make parallel vertical slices down almost to the bottom but not through.

It is easier to start in the middle and work outward.

Put the garnish in ice water to open up the fan.

See Photo Page 46

Butternut Squash Basket

"A tisket, a tasket" it's a butternut squash basket
to decorate your dining table.

Slice off a thin section from the bottom of the squash to form a stable base and remove the stem.

To make the handle make two long cuts ¾ of an inch apart halfway down the squash.

Make two short cuts on the sides and remove the two side sections. Use a knife to remove the pulp inside the handle.
Hollow out the inside of the basket with a melon baller.

Fill the basket with celery stalks, cucumber spears and carrot sticks.

See Photo Page 47

Yellow Squash Goose

Your guests will flock to the table when this silly goose is displayed.

Select a bright yellow crooked neck squash with a narrow curved neck.

Cut a vertical slice off the top of the neck of the squash.

Cut a vertical slice off each side of the squash and cut a thin slice off the bottom for stability.

Use the two slices to form the wings.

Fasten the wings to the body with toothpicks.

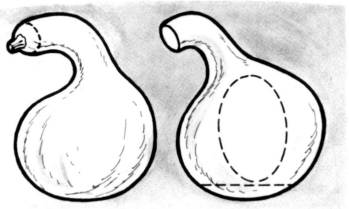

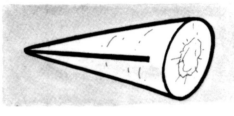

Carve a carrot into a cone shape to fit on the end of the neck.

Cut a horizontal slice to form the beak.

Fasten the carrot to the neck of the squash with a toothpick.

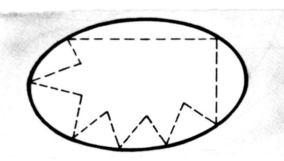

Carve the feet out of a slice of carrot.

Use cloves for the eyes.

Select different sizes of squash to form a parade.

See Photo Page 42

CHEF HARVEY

Turnip Bunny

Compliments will multiply when this Turnip Bunny hops on your table.

Select two turnips one larger than the other, peel and carve them into oval shapes.

Cut a ¼ inch slice from the bottom of the larger turnip and carve it into ears.

Cut a wedge at the front and insert the ears.
Insert cloves for the eyes.

Using a section cut from the smaller turnip, make the tail by cutting a series of slices close together ¾ of the way through.

Then turn the turnip 90 degrees and make another series of slices. Soak in ice water to curl the tail and attach with a tooth pick.

See Photo Page 42

HOW TO GARNISH

Tomato Butterfly

A bright red firm tomato makes an eye-pleasing garnish.

With the stem end down, cut a slice from the center of a firm tomato.

Cut this slice in half and peel 2/3 of the skin away from the pulp.

Arrange these to form the wings and antennae.

With each of the remaining sections make three even parallel cuts.

Make a cut in the center of the inner slices.
Spread these slices and place over the wings and antennae.

See Photo Page 43

CHEF HARVEY

Cherry Tomato Rose

Perk up even a "ho-hum" meal with these colorful tomato garnishes.

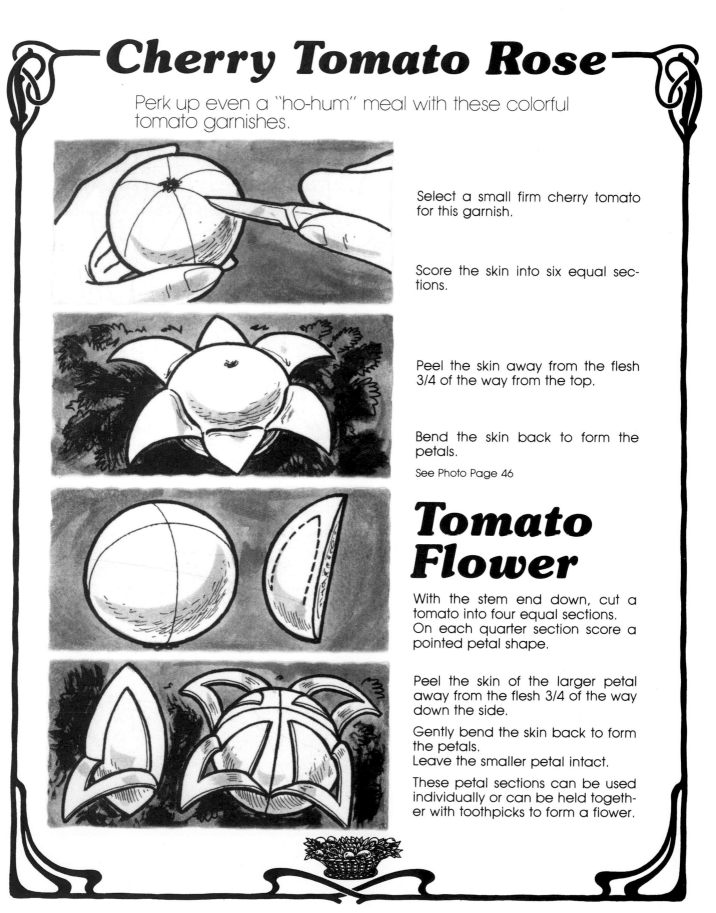

Select a small firm cherry tomato for this garnish.

Score the skin into six equal sections.

Peel the skin away from the flesh 3/4 of the way from the top.

Bend the skin back to form the petals.

See Photo Page 46

Tomato Flower

With the stem end down, cut a tomato into four equal sections. On each quarter section score a pointed petal shape.

Peel the skin of the larger petal away from the flesh 3/4 of the way down the side.

Gently bend the skin back to form the petals.
Leave the smaller petal intact.

These petal sections can be used individually or can be held together with toothpicks to form a flower.

Strip Tomato Rose

Brighten up a luncheon or any other meal with these easy-to-make tomato garnishes.

With a sharp paring knife peel the skin from a firm unblemished tomato.
Start at the stem end and continue peeling in one continuous strip 3/4 inch wide.
Remove as much flesh from the strip as possible.

Form a rose by rolling the strip in a tight coil, keeping the stem end to the outside.
Hold the rose together with a toothpick.

See Photo Page 34

Tomato Surprise

Select a large ripe tomato for this garnish.
Use a v-shaped food decorator or a sharp paring knife to form a zig-zag cut around the stem end.
Remove the top section and hollow out the tomato to make a shell.

Fill the shell with tuna, egg or chicken salad, cottage cheese, cooked carrots or peas.
Add a radish rose or an olive to complete the garnish.

See Photo Page 43 and 46

CHEF HARVEY

Tomato Wings

This garnish can also be made from a large cucumber, apple, citrus fruit or other round firm fruit.

Cut off the stem end of a very firm, well rounded tomato.

Using a sharp knife cut a small v wedge in the top of the tomato.

Continue making v wedges each a little larger than the previous one.

The number of wedges will depend upon the size of the tomato.

Separate ⅔ of the skin away from the flesh on each remaining section and fold it back.

Slide the v shaped sections forward, fanning them to form the central section.

See Photo Page 43

Vegetable Butterfly

The delicate vegetable butterfly adds an elegant touch to your dining table.

Cut a large slice ⅜ inch thick from a turnip, carrot or beet.
Make a cut 3/4 through the center of the slice.

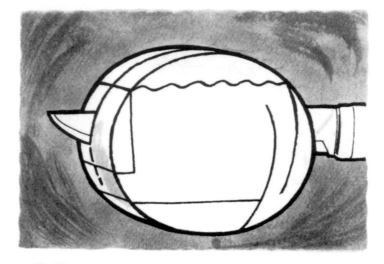

Use a corrugated garnishing tool to create a wavy edge across the top.
Make slices as shown.

Soak in salt water until pliable.
Separate the wings and tuck the front section in between the wings.
Soak in cold water.

For a colorful butterfly soak in food coloring.
Use a toothpick to support the butterfly.

See Photo Page 33 and 40

CHEF HARVEY

88

Candy Cane Vegetables

Candy cane vegetables are made from the curls cut by a twin curl cutter.

For the best results use large vegetables that are at room temperature.
Cold vegetables are brittle and tend to split.

Attach the handle to the end of the shaft of the tool and insert the point of the tool into the center of the vegetable.

When using beets or turnips, select those that are short and wide and insert the tool through the side, not the root end.

Press lightly and turn the tool clockwise.
Continue turning until the double rings cut through the other end of the vegetable.

Remove the handle and slide the shaft out the bottom.
To remove the curls from the vegetable, turn them clockwise; do not pull them.

The curls are used to make the candy cane vegetables and the hollowed section may be used to create stuffed vegetables.

To separate the two curls, turn them in opposite directions.
Intertwine curls from beets, carrots, turnips, and potatoes to produce candy cane vegetables.
Beet, turnip, and carrot curls may be simmered in lightly salted water for 8-10 minutes or pickled.

See Photo Page 35 and 45

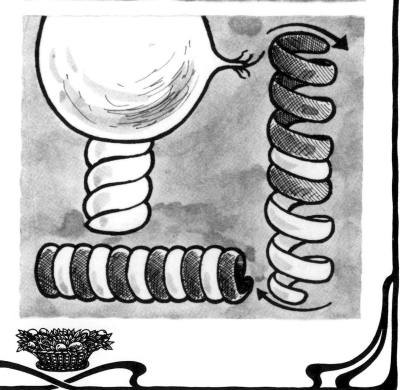

HOW TO GARNISH

Carved Rose

Select a fresh, unblemished turnip, beet, carrot, potato or other hard core vegetable for this garnish.

Holding the root end, make four connecting diagonal cuts into the side of the vegetable.

Carve a ring around the circumference behind the petals and remove the ring.

This forms the first row of petals.

To make more petals simply repeat the same steps but make the diagonal cuts in between the previous row of petals to give a floral effect.

The number of rows depends upon the size of the vegetable.

Soak the roses in ice water to open the petals further.

Potato roses can be deep fried or baked.

Roses can be made ahead of time and stored in ice water in the refrigerator until serving.

See Photo Page 47

Vegetable Chain

This garnish can be made from potatoes, beets, turnips, bright sweet potatoes or yams.

Cut a large vegetable lengthwise to make a 3/8 inch slice.

Square off the vegetable into a rectangular block.

With a very sharp paring knife, make parallel cuts evenly spaced all the way through the vegetable leaving a 1/4 inch border.

Use the blade of the knife to weave through every other cut.
If this is difficult to do soak the vegetable in warm water.
Cold vegetables are brittle and have a tendency to crack.
Slide the knife down and cut through the 1/4 inch border making sure not to cut through the links.
Turn the vegetable around and weave the blade of the knife through the cuts in the opposite direction.
Slide the knife down and cut through the other 1/4 inch border.

Separate the two interlocking sections.
Cut each of these sections in half by cutting through the center of the links.
Whittle the links until they are perfect.
Be careful not to cut through the cross bars.
Round off the corners by making small angular cuts.

Gently pull the links apart into a chain.
Soak the vegetable in lightly salted water for 5 minutes then drain.
Potato chains can be deep fried.

See Photo Page 35

Crinkle Cut

The proper tool turns ordinary vegetables into taste-tempting treats.

Use a corregated garnishing tool to make crinkle cut carrot sticks or french fries.

Waffle Cut

The waffle cut is made by slicing a vegetable with a corregated garnishing tool then giving it a half turn and slicing it again with the tool.
The slices should be made as thin as possible.
Waffle cuts can be made from carrots, potatoes or cucumbers.

Scallop Cut

A corregated garnishing tool can be used to create a wavy edge on vegetables.
Stand the vegetable up and trim the outside with the tool.
Cut in slices to make carrot, beet, potato, cucumber or turnip scallop slices.

See Photo Page 46

Vegetable Leaves

Vegetables such as carrots, turnips, cucumbers and beets can be converted into leaves to decorate flower garnishes.

Cut long thin vegetable slices.
Use a paring knife to form the jagged edge around the leaf.
Place three or four leaves together to give an added touch to a flower garnish.

See Photo Page 34

Cucumber Daisy

Cut a 1½ inch long section from the end of an unpeeled cucumber.
Scoop out the center with a melon baller to form a cup.
With a paring knife, scallop the edge of the cucumber to resemble petals.
Cut a slice from the bottom to provide a stable base.
Place in ice water for 10 minutes to open the petals.
Fill the cucumber with an olive, cherry tomato, tartar sauce or horseradish.

Spiral Vegetables

This garnish can be made from beets, turnips, carrots or potatoes.

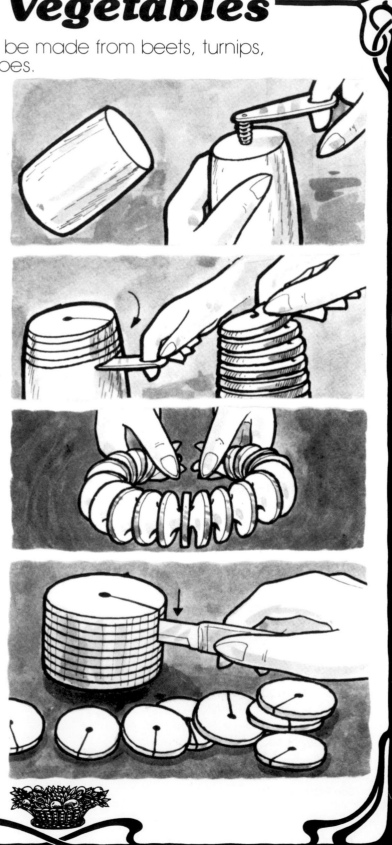

The vegetable should be at room temperature to prevent splitting.

Use a knife or a corrugated garnishing tool to cut the vegetable into a cylinder shape.

Insert the screw of the spiral slicer into the center of the top of the vegetable.

Place your finger into the hole and turn the tool clockwise.

As you turn the tool the screw will work its way through the vegetable and carve a spiral design.

Attach the ends of the spiral together with a toothpick.

The potato spiral can be fried.

Potato Chips

Potato chips, home fries, or cottage fries can be made from the spiral potato by cutting with a paring knife down the screw hole and making a single cut outward.

Separate the slices and fry to a golden brown.

See Photo Page 35

Vegetable Twigs

This decorative garnish can easily be made from celery, carrots or cucumbers.

Cut a section of the vegetable into a rectangular shape.

Make two lengthwise cuts from each side. (Making sure not to cut all the way through.)

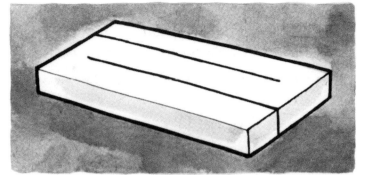

Soak in salted water until pliable. Twist the two outer ends on top of each other.

Cucumber Fan

For best results use a large, un-peeled cucumber.
Remove ½ of an inch off of one end.
Cut the cucumber in half length-wise.

Make evenly spaced, parallel slices through the cucumber one inch from the rounded end.

Soak the cucumber in salted water until it is flexible enough to be bent without cracking.

Fold every second strip toward the center to form the garnish as shown.

See Photo Page 46

HOW TO GARNISH

Zucchini Whale

A whale of a garnishing idea that is sure to be a conversation piece on your table.

For the best results select a large zucchini that is slightly curved.

Cut a ¼ inch slice from the bottom of the zucchini.

This piece is used later to make the tail.
Carve a wedge at the front to make the mouth.
Hollow out two holes, one on each side, for eyes and one at the top for the spout.
Carve out a slot half way into the zucchini at the back end.

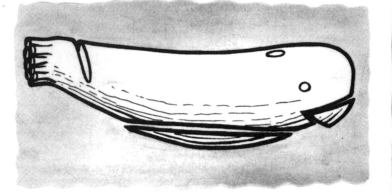

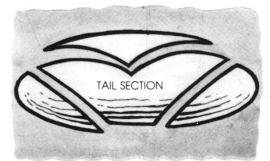

Using the piece cut from the bottom of the zucchini, shape the tail section as shown.
Insert this into the slot at the back.

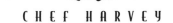

See Photo Page 41

Select a small scallion to make the spout.
Slice off the root end and make another slice approximately 4 inches from that.
Holding the scallion root end up, cut into the center of the scallion and make a slice approximately 1 inch down from the top.
Continue making these cuts all the way around the scallion.
Spin the vegetable to separate the cuts.
Insert this into the hole at the top of the zucchini.

CHEF HARVEY